Scrutinizing the Dust

poems by

Marjorie Hanft

Finishing Line Press
Georgetown, Kentucky

Scrutinizing the Dust

ACKNOWLEDGMENTS

Many thanks to the journals and anthologies in which the following poems first
appeared, a few in slightly different versions. Thanks also to the members of
the New York based online poetry group, Brevitas, from whom I have received
invaluable support.

Alte: "Unweave a Rainbow."
Brevitas 17: "Wild Persimmons Here & There," "After Sappho (in rural Illinois),"
"Note to Emily."
Brevitas 18: "Spring Catalog," "What It Must Be Like," "Arkansas," "In the Forest."
Calyx: "Leaving Oklahoma."
Cauldron Anthology (Issue 13- Maiden): "Color of the Hearth."
Eunoia Review: "After the Relapse"
First Literary Review East: "Trivia of Green," "First Color in Language," "World of
Dreams."
Graham House Review: "Portrait of Chaim Soutine."
Muddy River Poetry Review: "Poem Derived from an Article Called A Hungry
Cat," "More Light."
Persimmon Tree: "Light(s) at the End of the Tunnel," "After Hearing Eurydice on
the Radio (Metropolitan Opera)."
When We Turned Within: Reflections on Covid 19 (Edited by Rabbi Menachem
Creditor and Sarah Tuttle-Singer): "Poets to Read During a Pandemic"

Publisher: Leah Huete de Maines
Editor: Christen Kincaid
Cover Art: Deborah Hede
Author Photo: Amy Lynch
Cover Design: Elizabeth Maines McCleavy

Order online: www.finishinglinepress.com
also available on amazon.com

Author inquiries and mail orders:
Finishing Line Press
PO Box 1626
Georgetown, Kentucky 40324
USA

Contents

To my daughters, to Craig, to my brother, to the sisters I have been lucky to find in this world, and to the memory of Beloit College Professor of Classics, John Wyatt, who insisted that I learn to read Sappho if I wanted to write poetry and taught me how to translate Greek melic lyrics.

I know there is no straight road
No straight road in this world
Only a giant labyrinth
Of intersecting crossroads
—Federico Garcia Lorca

Leaving Oklahoma

Driving east   on a road lined
with split armadillos   their orange blood.
The baby in the back   leans forward
against her strap   small sounds cluck
in her throat because   she loves wind
eyelids droop fast   as if she knows
how hard the women   have tried
to be alone. Nearing the lake
that was theirs   once   when rain
kept hunters inside   dreaming they're
fading into   fall colors   fall coolness
the feel of rock   wrenched from sand.

The arm   of one woman is polished
rock against   the thigh of the other
streaks across their faces   are welts
of sand   as they remember & everything
begins to rise.   Hawks rise   pines rise
the blue that has been   so faithful   tilts
up & melts   into haze. But they are
sinking   into summer   the one with
the rock arm   is moving away

the other   waves her arm   at the sky
& they curve on   through convulsive
hills of Arkansas   two women   one child
on the torque   of a wind   that spins out
smells of sour wood   pressed
to paper   of skunk   in every stage
of decomposition   along the road.

Arkansas

It hovers   in the background of dreams   sinking into
its old   apartheid ways   swamps   emerald rice
fields   scarlet mold residue   which never completely
clears from toilet bowls.   Out of Barcelona   Ron Carter's
Spanish Blue   has a track named for it   after a child's misreading
of the name of a state   he'd never even seen.   It's the place
you never went back to   never even took   your firstborn to see
where you rocked her   through her first year.   It's not your wont
to think about   lush hills west of Little Rock   or a park called Toad
Suck   until there's   mild air in winter or a random nightmare
in which   some old Titan missile   gets nudged the wrong way.

Persimmons Wild & Everywhere

On the day you talk about   reading Homer aloud
I get to see you   eat a perfect persimmon
you've plucked from the ground   out of fallen leaves
as we hike through a grove   in the woods
surrounding the lake trail   marveling
at the fact that in the thirty   some odd years
you've lived here   this is your first time
tasting   the raw fruit   & knowing that in Greece
what are called date-plums are   bigger   softer
with smoother skin   & fewer seeds.   Only Odysseus
knows   what the lotus eaters ate   maybe *lotos*
Greek word   for the fruit   & largest berry there is.

After Sappho (in rural Illinois)

In praise of Adonis   in praise of Hera
one eye on the goldest
apple   perched too high

though at sunrise   arrows fly
dispersing deer   across the fields
of corn & beans   where
combines are   rasping lyres.

Weave dill   & wear
helichryse   dance the dance
of the Curetes   before you watch
a moonrise   before you spot
the Pleiades   before you sleep.

What It Must Be Like

There is a snapshot
taken roughly twelve years ago
from the top of Agua. It is probably
Pacaya or Fuego erupting.   At this
very moment you could be near
somewhere like this place
while I listen to rain
on my skylight at night
wondering what it must be like
to want to be that close to fire
day or night what you would
even want to do after that.

Winter Mishap

Day of the solstice   you missed the clear ice
on that steep   concrete boat ramp
yet stopped yourself from   sliding fast
into a freezing   blue lake. Broken humerus
& there's nothing humorous   about bruising
despite a hydrocodone buzz   or a tight sling
that would better fit   a one-breasted Amazon
though it holds in place   the slightly displaced
& fractured bone   from the quest   to see
herons.   Was it   really worth the risk? Younger
daughter notes   it's the second time   this lake has
tried   to take a parent   wonders   what she might
now need to sacrifice   to its sanguinary depths.

Valentine Unwrapped

No surefire way   to replicate complex
sweetness   or reinvent   the rapid flash
of a tang   in wintertime   grazing keen
but sensitive   outer edges   of the tongue.
Twinges sharp   & bittersweet   need
tweaking   with   blue agave nectar
plain old maple   syrup   fancy lavender
mango jam   or some other   kind of
treacly stuff.   The right amount of
cocoa   in the chili   or chili in the
cocoa   could change   everything.

Spring Catalog

Hail clap   thief ants   mangled sneaker
raccoon trap   turkey vulture   pelican rows
prairie fires   screeching crow. Ephemeral nights
violet leaves mourning cloaks pollen sneeze. *Wisconsin
death trip* ghostly maid   antique dresser   torn
brocade. Broken pencil   burnt s'mores   Dutchman's
breeches   forest floor flapping awning   slamming
door. Autumn olive   ripped sleeve   honeysuckle
hogweed   frosty morning   dripping eaves
hepatica   trillium   fractured sleep.

In the Forest

The begging cry
of a young   great horned owl
(with its tufts that look like
horns & eyes that don't
move) resounds from
the direction of the tallest
white pine
beyond the fire pit
interrupting
what was meant to be
a languid goodbye.

Sibling Hike at Warbler Ridge

Three days before Thanksgiving   fallen
oak leaves surround   skeletal asters
as we hike over ridges   down to
prairie   & the Embarrass (a tributary of
the Wabash   which is a tributary of the great
Ohio) & climb back up   eleven staircases
worth of ridges   & I fall behind
to take a photograph   of a bluebird
house   with a streak of sunlight beside it
that looks like   a spirit. My brother (binoculars
focused on two   redheaded woodpeckers
in a tree)   forges ahead.

Unweave a Rainbow

Emblem of a spectacular   incandescent   existential
childhood   we called her the prism lady   who babysat us
in her home   where we were   mesmerized
by a   lantern   or hurricane lamp   or were there crystals
dangling   from some Victorian lampshade   in that brick
house   in '60 or '61   when White Plains   was still a town where
a kid could   play in the woods   at the end of the street
never mind   hobos near the tracks   and were we already
on our own   submerged   in our latchkey days   when we were
put on that plane   to be with our Florida grandma   where
we   watched her neighbor   through the high rise   window
Lily   with her two-pronged   tushie poker   securing
as our destiny   a staunch belief   in witches?

Trivia of Green

Because who doesn't like   the symbol of spring
think chlorophyll in grass   & other things   that grow
and because it is restful   to the eyes
barium salts   are used to make   green sparks in fireworks.

Jade   emerald   malachite   hiddenite   peridot
my mother's eyes   but not mine she said
and I wasn't supposed   to wear her color either
as it represents   royalty   as in the cloth the Mona Lisa wears

& I want to believe it heals   because suicides   dropped
34% when London's   Blackfriars Bridge   was painted green
& there are always   viridescent fish   & birds
amphibians & reptiles   to imagine   surrounding
the pagan green man   of the woods   waiting at dusk
for that elusive   green flash   of sunset.

First Color in Language

After black and white   red is dear as purple
and as elegant   a color in most flags
and used to sell sex   though it is the international
sign for stop.   *Rubia tinctorum* is its plant   also called
the dyer's madder   and there are insects
like the cochineal   that manufacture the carmine
of lipstick.   My daughter painted the walls of her room
red   in high school   like the color of the big circle that is
the sun in the art of Japanese school children
as the red kimono stands for all the luck and joy I wish for her
my modern primitive   donner of black cloaks   of scars
that turn from crimson to the color of her own skin
& because her name   means first woman
she dances   through the end of the spectrum   of visible
light   dances through the hematite   & red ochre
on the cave art walls   of her dreams.

World of Dreams

Donovan tried to mellow it   but just couldn't resist
that *electrical banana*   & there's Zappa with his
don't you eat that yellow snow.   Never just   light
& bright   because there's the school bus   & the yield
sign   & the tint of jealousy   scattering its   weedy
dandelion   strands   all over the place. Amber
sweetgum leaves   outside my office window   in fall
once prompted me to   paint the walls   a color a friend
called   *Tibetan Buddhist gold.*   Locate   the meaning
of yellow   & you will find   that it blinks   & flickers
with intuitive intellect   in the REM   world of dreams.

Impression Orange

There are languages   with no precise word
for orange   which Kandinsky called   *red brought nearer*
to humanity by yellow. It came to English   by way of Sanskrit
& the Persian *naranjee*   the word for the fruit   & it is
a daughter's   aural memory   that made her language
meaningful   *echolalic wholes*   strung together
by accident & intuition.   When she understands
what she reads   you can see in her face   in her
sudden direct gaze   she's   the essence
of Monet's   sunrise   reflected in water.

Portrait of Chaim Soutine

Wandered   like a Jew   wanders
shy   with a temper   loving no one
sleepwalking   counting Cossacks   waking
alone with garnets in his hair.   Thrown
out of   the Russian ghetto   for asking
the rebbe   to pose   twenty-five rubles
restitution & dream.   In Paris   neighbors
shrieked   at the black-eyed man   who painted
sides of beef   his pale hands dribbling blood.

Maggots   crawled around   the stinking room
where he refused   to draw nudes   confessing
to his friend Modigliani   who reeled   laughing
everything dances around me like a landscape
by Soutine mother-of-pearl   amber   emerald

pastry chefs & hanging fowl   choirboys
& tilted streets   paved with sapphires.   Gut
ruptured at forty-nine   he closed his charcoal
eyes   on canvasses torn   & stashed in cupboards
in Minsk   on two days of hunger   in the cellar
for pawning   his mama's skillets   for crayons.

Color of the Hearth

White foxes   the ermine   beluga whales
know nothing of   leukophobia   (the human fear
of the color white) along with   a fear of ghosts
phantoms   the specter of a woman in white
commonly seen   by those who see such things.

White is like no color   achromatic   supposed
consistency of sunlight   or chalk   acquiring
a tinge of blue   like breast milk   or glaciers
or it's a chaste white   underwear & bedsheets
white of the 18th century   & so many women's
names are derived from   white flowers   & pearls.

(No one should get married   as I did
sporting a tiara of   white roses   as if equipped
to impersonate   the Statue of Liberty   wearing
a gown   & carrying   a torch-like nosegay.)

A more austere white   *blanc cassé*   was worn
by women   immediately after   the French
Revolution   white   also a sign of reincarnation
& the tone   of linen robes   veils   and shawls
of the priestesses   of Hestia (also called Vesta)
those guardians of   the sacred hearth.

More Light

I've been thinking   about the day   in August
when my mother died   which just happens to be
Goethe's birthday.   Poetry was   not what he was
proud of   but the science of color   an iron oxide
named for him.   My mother liked to paint
and there's her   painting of a yellow building
beside a palm tree   blue sky   white puff
clouds   on a wall in my home.   Did free
thinker Goethe   really ask   for more light
when he died?   Who knows?   He said   blue
deepens   *mildly into* red   & on his color
wheel   it's yellow that's   face to face with blue.

Note to Emily

My dear   *nearer here*   does not jibe
with my sense   of geography (**Vesuvius
at home**   is nothing like what I need)   & it
was enough   to land in this town   & dream
about an earthquake   in Mexico while
it was   happening.   If I must
have   a sightedness   I didn't choose
then lend me   your old dresser
drawer.   What I'm prompted   to jot
down   might be better off   socked away
beneath   a threadbare   nightgown.

Poem Derived from an Article Called A Hungry Cat

(Journal of Geological Education, 1994)

Old places   rocks   food   men doing what they like to do
in the company of a cat   men who like to climb   who spit
on coccoliths   scrutinize the dust   of the universe
in Perugia   or anywhere   indifferent to the fact that   the cats of Italy
are Egyptian imports   quick though to notice   when a greeting
announces   the wrong time of day   or when a chicken dish can't be
replicated   yet can be shared   with a stray   who then finds
it easy   to sleep   paws crossed   & tucked underneath.

Tribute to Dust

Even your thoughts are dust. -Lucinda Williams

Dust up   dust down
dust your pants   dust to dust
dust my broom   gather dust
kiss the dust   eat my dust
dust of   everyday life.

Raise dust   smart dust
as dry as dust   watch my dust
desert dust   diamond dust
immortal & amorphous dust
throw dust   in someone's eyes.

Poets to Read During a Pandemic

Yeats   for the love of   flapping herons   & for more
weeping than the world   can understand   even
at this time   & Sexton for believing   there will come a time
when it's okay for kids   to pick gum   off the sidewalk
again   & Derek Walcott   even though   you could never
ever be   that stranger   who has loved yourself   your whole life
& because   at the beginning   of a reading   he once said to his
audience   *when you give a reading   basically   you wish that*
nobody was there   so will you please leave   & Jean Valentine
because   if someone you know   visits you in a dream
you almost always   have the urge   to tell them about it.

After Hearing *Eurydice* on the Radio (Metropolitan Opera)

She has crossed the river   of forgetfulness   only to find herself
in a shower in the elevator   that takes her down   to the Underworld
no memory   no words   & she doesn't know who her father is
though in my case   I wonder how long it will be   before my dad
doesn't know   who I am   because yesterday   after I walked around
him   after sundown   to retrieve my phone   he didn't even know
I was there   because sundowning is a real thing.   Can a man whose
message   is delivered by a worm   restore memory?   Meanwhile
which Orpheus   is which   & is it even possible   to meet someone
interesting   anymore?   My father takes   a new dip   each day into
the river   of forgetfulness   & why   even when the title is   *Eurydice*
must everything   always   turn out to be   so orphic   in the end?

After the Relapse

She talks about   not getting   out
of bed   not moving   just sitting   inside
the music   she can't quite hear   returning
to men   & women   she didn't even   want to know.

I woke up   in a junked car   on Railroad Street
that winter morning   clothes   gone
& no way   to get home.   Should have seen that
coming   felt   feather light   for days
as if   my feet   had left   the frozen ground.

She just wants to put   one foot   in front of
the other again   to know how   to stay
on track   how to ask   for directions
even   when she's sure   she knows the way.

Light(s) at the End of the Tunnel

There must be a reason   I'd rather listen to women
poets these days   Valentine mentioned   *strange lights*

beyond   the hospital room (may her memory
be   for a blessing).   Lowell saw   only the train

& Bukowski   was all about how   *there isn't even
a tunnel.*   Rukeyser   on the other hand   always

saw the tunnel   believing   no one   ever needed
to stand inside.   If you   do happen   to hang out

in the tunnel   of oblivion   festive illuminants
could be strung   from one end   to the other.

Marjorie Hanft taught psychology for 27 years at Eastern Illinois University (until retirement in 2015). She continues to live in rural Illinois, caring for her centenarian dad with the help of her partner, a geologist, and hiking in local conservation areas. Her two adult daughters live nearby. Hanft's poems have appeared in such journals as *Alte, Calyx, Cauldron Anthology, First Literary Review-East, Graham House Review, Humana Obscura, Muddy River Poetry Review, Persimmon Tree*, and various anthologies.